anythink

D0554889

THE BEST
DOGS
EVER

POODLES
ARE THE
BEST!

Elaine Landau

LERNER PUBLICATIONS COMPANY · MINNEAPOLIS

For Loretta Dowell

Lerner Publications Company
A division of Lerner Publishing Group, Inc.
241 First Avenue North
Minneapolis, MN 55401 U.S.A.

Website address: www.lernerbooks.com

Library of Congress Cataloging-in-Publication Data

Landau, Elaine.
    Poodles are the best! / by Elaine Landau.
        p. cm. — (The best dogs ever)
    Includes index.
    ISBN 978-1-58013-561-0 (lib. bdg. : alk. paper)
    1. Poodles—Juvenile literature. I. Title.
    SF429.P85L36 2010
    636.72'8—dc22   2008046792

Manufactured in the United States of America
1 – BP – 12/15/09

TABLE OF CONTENTS

CHAPTER ONE

YOUR POODLE PAL

Delightful to hold.
Lovely to see.
I'm easy to train,
'cause I'm smart as can be.

Have you ever looked at a happy, healthy poodle? Could this be what it's thinking? These super dogs have made their owners proud for years. In fact, the poodle's good looks and keen intelligence have made it one of the most popular dog breeds in the United States!

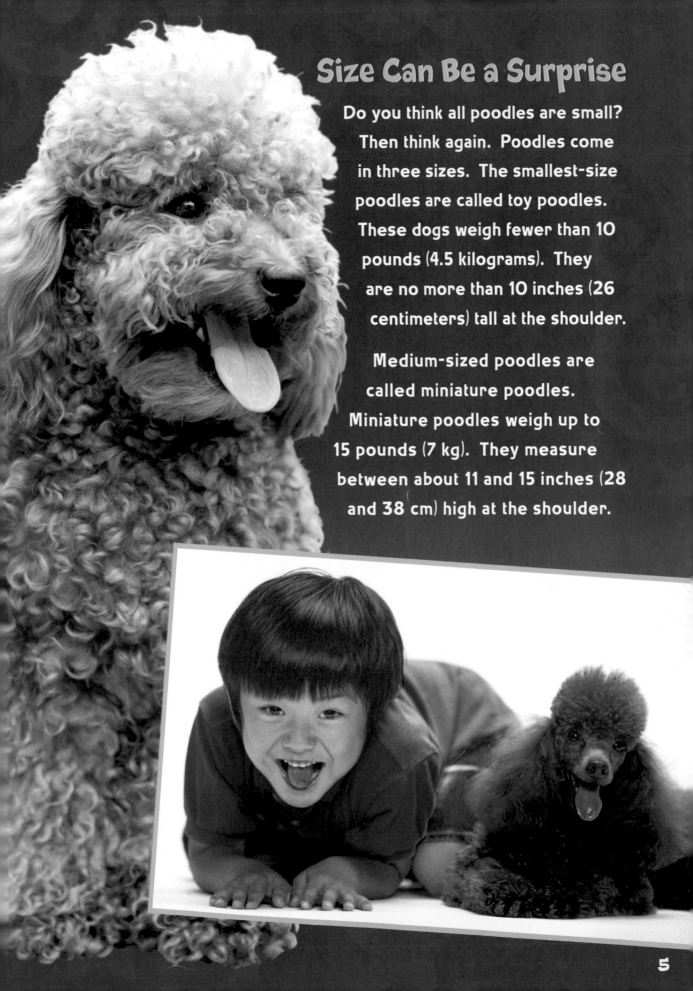

Size Can Be a Surprise

Do you think all poodles are small? Then think again. Poodles come in three sizes. The smallest-size poodles are called toy poodles. These dogs weigh fewer than 10 pounds (4.5 kilograms). They are no more than 10 inches (26 centimeters) tall at the shoulder.

Medium-sized poodles are called miniature poodles. Miniature poodles weigh up to 15 pounds (7 kg). They measure between about 11 and 15 inches (28 and 38 cm) high at the shoulder.

The biggest poodles are called standard poodles. These are large, graceful dogs. Some are as tall as 28 or even 30 inches (71 or 76 cm) high at the shoulder. They weigh between 45 and 55 pounds (20 and 25 kg). That's about as much as a five- or six-year-old child.

Colorful Pooches

Poodles are like a rainbow. They come in many colors. You can find gray, black, apricot, cream, and white poodles.

Some poodles are a color called café au lait. In French, *café au lait* means "coffee mixed with milk." And that's just what café au lait looks like! It is a light brownish color.

This standard poodle has a café au lait coat.

PARTI-COLOR POODLES

Poodles whose coats are more than one color are called parti-color poodles. These dogs might be black and white, gray and white, black and apricot, or a number of other color combinations. Parti-color poodles do not meet the breed standard. This means they don't match up with the guidelines that are used to judge poodles in dog shows. For this reason, parti-color poodles cannot compete in shows. But they make great pets.

A Fun Friend

Poodles are fun to be around. These dogs like being around people too. Their owners often say poodles have a sense of humor. They make you smile.

Many poodles learn to do tricks. Some can even jump through hoops and dance on their hind legs. Well-behaved poodles often do quite well in dog shows.

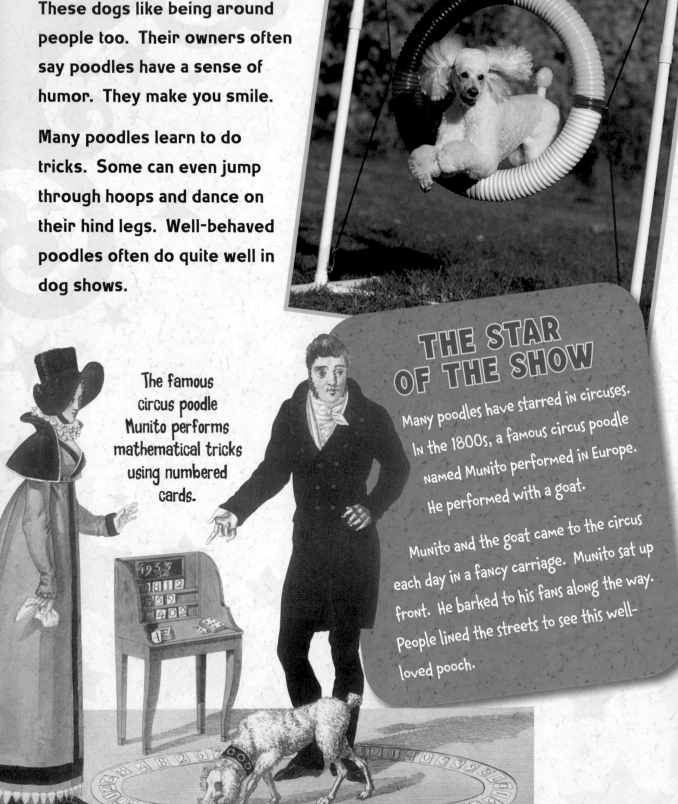

The famous circus poodle Munito performs mathematical tricks using numbered cards.

THE STAR OF THE SHOW

Many poodles have starred in circuses. In the 1800s, a famous circus poodle named Munito performed in Europe. He performed with a goat.

Munito and the goat came to the circus each day in a fancy carriage. Munito sat up front. He barked to his fans along the way. People lined the streets to see this well-loved pooch.

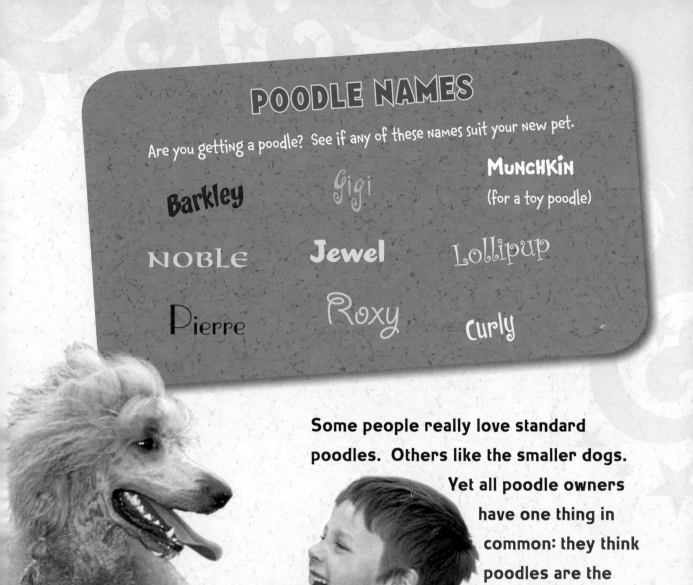

POODLE NAMES

Are you getting a poodle? See if any of these names suit your new pet.

Barkley

Gigi

Munchkin
(for a toy poodle)

NOBLE

Jewel

Lollipup

Pierre

Roxy

Curly

Some people really love standard poodles. Others like the smaller dogs. Yet all poodle owners have one thing in common: they think poodles are the best dogs ever!

CHAPTER TWO

ALL ABOUT POODLES

Have you ever heard of a French poodle? If so, you might think that poodles come from France. These pooches are France's national dog, after all.

But many people think the poodle got its start in Germany. Poodles were living in Germany as far back as the early fifteenth century. The dogs made loyal companions to many families there.

A woman plays with her pet poodle in a French painting from 1740.

This 1803 illustration shows a poodle fetching a stick.

Oodles of Poodles Hard at Work

No matter where poodles come from, one thing is certain: poodles were once very hard workers. In the 1500s, large poodles helped hunters in Germany. These dogs were water retrievers. Water retrievers go into lakes and ponds to retrieve—or bring back—birds that hunters kill for food.

A poodle practices for hunting by retrieving a toy duck.

The Germans called their water retrievers Pudels. This name came from the German word *pudeln*. *Pudeln* means "to splash"—something poodles did a lot of when they were retrieving birds!

WHY THE FANCY HAIRCUT?

Perhaps you've seen a poodle that had its legs and hind end shaved. These dogs have poofy fur on their chests and big tufts of fur near their paws. You may have thought the poodle's haircut looked kind of funny. But there's a good reason for that fancy do!

The poodle's haircut began as a way to help it work in water. Poodles' thick, curly coats become quite heavy when wet. So retrieving poodles were shaved to make their fur lighter. This helped the dogs swim more easily. The hair on the poodles' ankles, chest, and head was left in place to help keep the dogs warm.

Smaller poodles also worked. They were trained as truffle dogs. Truffles are a fancy kind of mushroom. They grow underground in the woods. Truffle dogs sniffed out the truffles and dug them up.

Truffles like these are hard to find. They grow underground.

White poodles made especially good truffle dogs. Why? People usually looked for truffles at night. White dogs were easiest to see after dark!

A woman watches as her poodle hunts for truffles. Some poodles still sniff out truffles in modern times.

A Great Breed

Today the American Kennel Club (AKC) groups purebred dogs by breed. Some of the AKC's groups include the herding group, the working group, and the sporting group. Standard and miniature poodles are in the nonsporting group.

This boxer belongs to the working group.

Border collies belong to the herding group.

Springer spaniels, like this one, are in the sporting group.

Bulldogs are part of the nonsporting group.

The nonsporting group is made up of many different kinds of dogs. They do not look very much alike. Yet they are all squarely built and sturdy. Some other dogs in the nonsporting group include the bulldog and the chow chow.

WONDERFUL WESTMINSTER WINNERS!

Over the years, nine poodles have won Best in Show at the famous Westminster Kennel Club Dog Show. Here's a look at a few:

• In 1956, a white toy poodle named Wilber White Swan won. Known as Peanuts at home, this splendid pooch wowed the Westminster judges with his spirit and style.

• In 1991, a standard poodle called Whisperwind's On A Carousel snatched the title. Also known as Peter, this dog won Best in Show 101 times at different dog shows!

• A three-year-old miniature poodle named Surrey Spice Girl (right) won Westminster's Best in Show title in 2002. After winning, this pretty poodle retired from the show ring and had some great-looking puppies.

FIT FOR A KING

Royals have long loved poodles. King Louis XVI of France had pet poodles. So did Prince Rupert of Germany.

Rupert's small white poodle was always with him. The dog slept in his bed and ate at the royal table. Rupert fed his pooch roast beef out of his hand.

In this 1643 illustration, Prince Rupert charges into battle with his poodle. The dog's name was Boye.

Toy poodles are in the toy group. Dogs in this group are very small. Other dogs in the toy group are the Maltese and the pug.

CHAPTER THREE

ARE YOU A POODLE PERSON?

Poodles have lots of pluses. They are beautiful as well as friendly. They are great people pleasers too.

Having a smart dog can be super, and poodles are supersmart. If these dogs went to school, they'd earn great grades! Their smarts help them quickly learn to make their owners happy.

DESIGNER DOGS

First, there were designer shoes. Then came designer jeans. Now we have designer dogs! A designer dog is a mix between two purebred dog breeds. A schnoodle (left) is a designer dog. It's a mix between a schnauzer and a poodle. Schnoodles weigh between 10 and 15 pounds (4.5 and 7 kg). They are both smart and good-natured.

Another good thing about poodles is that these dogs don't shed. This is not true of most dogs. You can pet your poodle and not be covered in dog hair. People with allergies often do well with poodles. Some allergy sufferers say that poodles are the only dogs they can be around.

Is a Poodle Right for You?

Since poodles come in three sizes, some people say there's a poodle for everyone. But this isn't always so.

If you're looking for a guard dog, don't get a poodle. Your poodle may bark to let you know that someone is coming. Just don't expect it to be an attack dog. These dogs are too friendly for that job.

There are other things to think about as well. If you get a poodle, you may be teased. This may be partly because of poodles' fancy haircuts.

Sadly, some people don't understand these terrific dogs. They think of poodles as stuck up or "sissy" dogs. Nothing could be farther from the truth! But still, dog owners need to be proud of their pooch. Would you feel good walking down the street with a poodle? If not, another dog might be better for you.

Do you have time for a poodle? Poodles need to be petted, played with, and praised every day. Large poodles need lots of exercise. They like long walks. Some fun in the park is a good idea too.

Even tiny toy poodles will want to do more than sit in your lap. Don't let their size fool you. These dogs like being active. They enjoy playing fetch and other games. A bored or lonely poodle will not be happy. At times, this may lead to bad behavior. Then you and your family won't be happy either.

A CHANNEL-SURFING DOG!

Beware of the bored poodle. One poodle did not like being ignored while her owner watched TV. So she found a way around this. The dog would pick up the remote with her mouth. Then she'd use her paw to change the channel!

Poodles need lots of exercise.

Good Grooming

You've probably seen poodles with lovely, fluffy coats. These dogs don't look that way on their own. Poodles need lots of grooming.

Poodles must be brushed and combed regularly. Their coats and nails also need to be trimmed often. You can take your poodle to a groomer. Just remember that this can get costly. And in between trips to the groomer, you'll still have to groom your poodle at home.

A professional groomer will help your poodle look its best.

Be honest with yourself before getting a new dog. Are you willing to do what it takes to have a poodle? Can you be a responsible pet owner? If so, get set to welcome a wonderful dog home.

A poodle can be the perfect pet if you're willing to take good care of it!

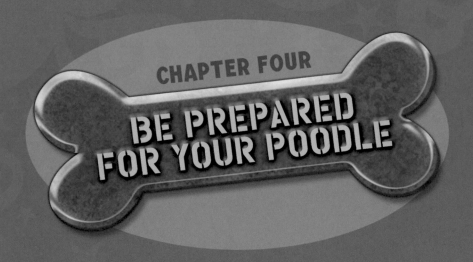

CHAPTER FOUR

BE PREPARED FOR YOUR POODLE

Today is the big day. You are bringing home your new poodle. It's going to be a day you'll never forget.

Have your camera ready. You'll want pictures. And make sure to stock up on pet supplies too.

Not sure what you'll need to welcome Fido to your family? This basic list is a great place to start:

- collar

- leash

- tags (for identification)

- dog food

- food and water bowls

- crates (one for when your pet travels by car and one for it to rest in at home)

- treats (to be used in training)

- toys

PURE POODLE PLEASURE

Having fun with your poodle doesn't have to cost a lot. Try this: Put a tennis ball inside an old sock. Knot the sock above the ball, and give it to your dog. Watch your poodle have a ball!

Visit Your Vet

A veterinarian, or vet, is a doctor who treats animals. Take your poodle to a vet right away. The vet will check your pet's health. The vet will also give your dog any shots it needs. This will help keep your poodle well.

TAILS TELL TALES

Watch your poodle's tail. It should stand up straight. When your poodle is afraid or sick, its tail will droop.

You may want to ask your vet what to feed your poodle. Different foods are made for dogs and puppies. Your vet will know what's best for your dog.

Time with Your Poodle

Plan to spend some extra time with your poodle in the first few days after you adopt it. Your pet is in a new home with new people. Make it feel happy and comfortable.

If your new poodle is a puppy, you'll also need to housebreak it. It should learn some basic commands too. Everyone loves a well-behaved dog.

A well-trained poodle will be welcome everywhere.

FURRY SNACK FOOD!

Poodles can learn to get along with other pets. It is best to introduce them to other dogs or cats while they are young. That way, they can get used to being around the other animals.

However, you should never leave your poodle alone with a small pet like a gerbil or hamster. These furry little guys may mean a lot to you. Yet your poodle may just see them as a tasty treat. Always keep these pets in a cage out of your dog's reach.

Poodles are wonderful dogs. They make loving pets. Some poodle owners even claim that their poodles can read their minds! That's not likely to be true—yet poodles and their owners do often become unusually close. You and your poodle will soon be best friends.

Show your poodle how much you adore it. Be the best dog owner you can be. Your dog will bring you years of joy in return.

GLOSSARY

American Kennel Club (AKC): an organization that groups dogs by breed. The AKC also defines the characteristics of different breeds.

breed: a particular type of dog. Dogs of the same breed have the same body shape and general features.

coat: a dog's fur

groom: to clean, brush, and trim a dog's coat

miniature poodle: a medium-sized poodle. Miniature poodles weigh up to 15 pounds (7 kg) and measure between about 11 and 15 inches (28 and 38 cm) tall at the shoulder.

nonsporting group: a group of many different types of dogs that are squarely built and sturdy. Dogs in the nonsporting group generally lack the characteristics of hunting dogs.

purebred: a dog whose parents are of the same breed

shed: to lose fur

standard poodle: the largest-size poodle. Standard poodles weigh between 45 and 55 pounds (20 and 25 kg) and measure as much as 30 inches (76 cm) tall at the shoulder.

toy group: a group of different types of dogs that are all small in size

toy poodle: the smallest-size poodle. Toy poodles weigh fewer than 10 pounds (4.5 kg) and are no more than 10 inches (26 cm) tall at the shoulder.

veterinarian: a doctor who treats animals. Veterinarians are called vets for short.

water retriever: a dog that goes into lakes and ponds to retrieve, or bring back, birds that hunters kill for food

FOR MORE INFORMATION

Books

Brecke, Nicole, and Patricia M. Stockland. *Dogs You Can Draw*. Minneapolis: Millbrook Press, 2010. This colorful book shows how to draw different kinds of dogs, including the poodle, and shares fun facts about each breed.

Goldish, Meish. *Toy Poodle: Oodles of Fun*. New York: Bearport: 2009. If you love small poodles, check out this book all about the tiniest dogs in the poodle family.

Landau, Elaine. *Yorkshire Terriers Are the Best!* Minneapolis: Lerner Publications Company, 2010. Read all about the Yorkshire terrier—another fabulous dog breed!

Sjonger, Rebecca, and Bobbie Kalman. *Puppies*. New York: Crabtree, 2004. Find out what you need to know about picking out and caring for a puppy in this book. Information on visiting the veterinarian is also included.

Wheeler, Jill C. *Labradoodles*. Edina, MN: Abdo, 2008. Learn about designer dogs called Labradoodles—a mix between poodles and Labrador retrievers.

Websites

American Kennel Club
http://www.akc.org
Visit this website to find a complete listing of AKC-registered dog breeds, including the poodle. The site also features fun printable activities for kids.

ASPCA Animaland
http://www2.aspca.org/site/PageServer?pagename=kids_pc_home
Check out this page for helpful hints on caring for a dog and other pets.

Index

Photo Acknowledgments

The images in this book are used with the permission of: © iStockphoto.com/Ruth Ann Johnston, p. 4; © Xiaweiqing/Dreamstime.com, p. 5 (left); © D-BASE/Photodisc/Getty Images, p. 5 (right); © artparadigm/Digital Vision/Getty Images, p. 6; © P. Wegner/Peter Arnold, Inc., pp. 6-7; © Mark Raycroft/Minden Pictures, p. 8 (top); © Mary Evans Picture Library/Everett Collection, p. 8 (bottom); © tbkmedia.de/Alamy, p. 9; © INTERFOTO/Alamy, p. 10; © Mary Evans Picture Library/ The Image Works, p. 11 (top); © Jerry Shulman/SuperStock, pp. 11 (bottom), 14 (center), 25 (bottom); © iStockphoto.com/david kahn, p. 12 (top); © Kendall McMinimy/Photographer's Choice/Getty Images, p. 12 (bottom); © Zirafek/Dreamstime.com, p. 13 (top); © Peter Frischmuth/Peter Arnold, Inc., p. 13 (bottom); © Eric Isselée/Dreamstime.com, pp. 14 (left), 16 (bottom); © Eric Isselée/Shutterstock Images, pp. 14 (right), 15 (top); AP Photo/Ron Frehm, p. 15 (bottom); © HIP/Art Resource, NY, p. 16 (top); © age fotostock/SuperStock, pp. 17, 19, 20 (main); © Dewayne Flowers/Shutterstock Images, p. 18 (top); © iStockphoto.com/a-wrangler, p. 18 (bottom); © Pam Francis/Photographer's Choice/ Getty Images, p. 20 (inset); © John Terence Turner/Photographer's Choice/Getty Images, p. 21; © Dorling Kindersley/Getty Images, p. 22 (top); © iStockphoto.com/aldra, p. 22 (bottom); © Dan Hallman/Photodisc/Getty Images, p. 23 (left); © Ldeavila/Dreamstime.com, p. 23 (right); © Yoshio Tomil/SuperStock, p. 24; © Tooties/Dreamstime.com, p. 25 (top); © Uturnpix/Dreamstime.com, p. 25 (second from top); © iStockphoto.com/orix3, p. 25 (third from top); © Jaimie Duplass/Shutterstock Images, p. 26 (top); © Johan Bonde Ferm/Dreamstime.com, p. 26 (bottom); © iStockphoto.com/ Monique Rodriguez, p. 27; © iStockphoto.com/Leslie Banks, p. 28 (top); © MBWTE Photos/ Shutterstock Images, p. 28 (bottom); © iStockphoto.com/Greg Nicholas, pp. 28-29.

Front cover: © Juniors Bildarchiv/Alamy.
Back cover: © Eric Isselée/Dreamstime.com.